I0099281

Journey to Connecting with God

A Book of Devotionals

Angela Evans

Journey to Connecting with God: A Book of
Devotionals
Copyright © 2019 by Angela Evans

ISBN: 978-0-9981103-5-6

Library of Congress Control Number:
2019912068

Edited by Renita L. Webb

Cover Design by Drake Creative

Published by Semaj Publishing

Printed in the United States of America

All rights reserved under the International
Copyright Law. Contents and/or cover may
not be reproduced in whole or in part in any
form without the express written consent of
the Publisher.

This book is available at special discounts
for churches, schools, community
organizations, and educational institutions.

Contact Semaj Publishing
201-243-3700

Author Booking and Management
lfmanagementgroup@gmail.com

Introduction

Like so many others, I didn't fully understand how to trust God early in life. But now, as an adult, I realize how vital it is to keep faith in God. I am grateful for all the things that have transpired in my life which have helped me desire to seek God for myself. In seeking God I established a relationship with Him. I had to get to know Him for myself. Discovering what I have learned about God for myself enables me to have a better understanding of the reasons He allows us to experience trials and tribulations on Earth.

Knowing that God will never give me more than I can bear gives me the ability to see him in the midst of storms.

The journey was not easy to get to this place of peace in God. But now that I have developed the ability to navigate through life by referencing God's Word, I desire to inspire others to connect with God's Word in the same way.

The Bible tells us that there is nothing new under the sun. This means that every trial or tribulation that we are experiencing, someone else has already overcome. This fact should give us all hope and keep up optimism despite what we're experiencing.

My hope and prayer are that this 30-day book of devotionals will act as an aide to guide and encourages the reader to reference God's Word in their everyday experiences and quest to find God's Peace on earth.

Prayerfully,
Angela Evans

Trust in the LORD with all thine heart; and lean not unto thine own understanding. In all thy ways acknowledge him, and he shall direct thy paths.
Proverbs 3:5-6

Chapter 1
God is Our Creator

Day 1

"And without faith it is impossible to please God, because anyone who comes to him must believe that he exists and that he rewards those who earnestly seek him."

Hebrews 11:6

Knowing God is vital for survival! There would be no way to see past our trials if we did not know and have faith in God.

Just as important as it is to know and have faith in God is to stand on His promises; especially whenever we are experiencing challenges. Standing on the promises of God allows us to know that if we keep seeking Him, He will take care of us. That gives us solace.

Prayer:

Lord, please continue to keep our minds on you so that we never lose hope whenever we are faced with challenges.

Father, we love you and trust that you will always take care of us. In Jesus' name we pray, Amen.

Day 2

*"Before I formed you in the womb I knew
you, before you were born I set you apart;
I appointed you as a prophet to the nations."*
Jeremiah 1:5

God is our Creator. He knows all, controls all, and can do all things. God is not surprised by anything that is taking place on Earth. In fact, God warned us about the things that are occurring. So, don't look at the state of the world or even your life and ever think God doesn't know what is going on.

God created us for this specific time. It's no coincidence that we are seeking God's face for instructions and direction. He knew and knows what life holds for us. He knew the exact moment when we would be ready to serve and represent him before we were born.

We should have peace in the fact that He knew us before we were even born. He knew the things we would do and decided that He would remain with us always!

Prayer:

Lord, thank you for knowing us better than we know ourselves. Father, as we witness all of the acts of evil being done around us, we can't help but thank you for calling us out of darkness for a time such as this. Lord, continue to keep our minds in perfect peace as we continue to seek Your face. In Jesus' name we pray, Amen.

Day 3

"So do not fear, for I am with you; do not be dismayed, for I am your God. I will strengthen you and help you; I will uphold you with my righteous right hand."
Isaiah 41:10

As we witness all the acts of evil on earth, we must stay in His presence as much and as often as we can. This will limit the wavering of our faith. God knows that the enemy is always on the attack and seeking to destroy and devour His people. When it appears too much for you to handle, remember that God wants us to stand with total confidence and rely totally on His strength not our own. God has His hand of protection all around us.

Prayer:

Father, thank You for building up our faith in You. Lord, continue to strengthen us so that we never grow fearful and/or weary whenever the enemy attacks. In Jesus' name we pray, Amen.

Day 4

"Be strong and courageous. Do not be afraid or terrified because of them, for the L*ORD your God goes with you; he will never leave you nor forsake you."*

Deuteronomy 31:6

As believers we will constantly experience challenges that will test our faith. Don't let those stories be the ones you tell. God's Word reminds us to boldly testify about Him. Testifying is simply sharing our experiences with others. We are God's representatives on Earth. Whenever we share our testimonies we are identified as God's Followers on earth.

Prayer:

Lord, thank You for revealing Yourself to us and for building up our confidence in You. Lord, we trust in you and we know that you will always fight our battles. In Jesus' name we pray, Amen.

Day 5

"Ah, Sovereign LORD, you have made the heavens and the earth by your great power and outstretched arm. Nothing is too hard for you."
Jeremiah 32:17

It's so good to know that our God is Sovereign and we can do anything through His power. God is the Ultimate Supreme Being and there is no one who has close to His power. We are connected to God; He strengthens us and we are empowered as long as we activate that connection.

We have limitations in the things we can do with our human strength, but with God, we can do and accomplish anything that is in His will for our lives. God is so AWESOME!

Prayer:

Lord, thank You for blessing our lives with Your presence and for pouring Your grace and mercy upon us. Lord, thank You for blessing us with Your strength in our times of trouble. In Jesus' name we pray, Amen.

Day 6

"Yours, LORD, is the greatness and the power and the glory and the majesty and the splendor, for everything in heaven and earth is yours.

Yours, LORD, is the kingdom; you are exalted as head over all."
1 Chronicles 29:11

God is so AMAZING!

Acknowledging and expressing our gratefulness to God becomes automatic after we have a real encounter with Him. Prior to getting to know God, losing hope or getting frustrated whenever we had trials or tribulations was easy and at times finite. God's grace and mercy on us gives us the ability to see past our challenges. This is why it's easier for believers to speak about God's greatness despite what we are experiencing. Testifying about God's peace in the midst of our storms comes naturally because we would rather talk about our blessings than to dwell over our issues.

We should always be careful not to ever overlook or downplay God's Awesomeness!

God deserves our worship!

Glory to His Name!

Prayer:

Lord, You reign above everything on Earth. We reverence you in all that we do because you are so worthy to be praised. Lord, we love you and will always be careful to give you all the glory and honor all the days of our lives. In Jesus' name we pray, Amen.

Day 7

"For since the creation of the world God's invisible qualities—his eternal power and divine nature—have been clearly seen, being understood from what has been made, so that people are without excuse."

Romans 1:20

Whenever we think of life in its simplest form, we must admit that it's relieving to know that we do not have to worry about everything that's going on in this world.

Count it a blessing to be aware that God is all-powerful! We must have faith and rest in the peace knowing that God is very capable of handling all the cares of the world. God reigns supreme on Earth.

Prayer:
Father God, thank You for revealing Yourself to us. We realize that we could still be wandering in the wilderness unaware of Your divine nature, majesty and power. Thank You for being so astounding! In Jesus' name we pray, Amen.

*******REMINDER*******

"Though the mountains be shaken and the hills be removed, yet my unfailing love for you will not be shaken, nor my covenant of peace be removed", says the Lord, who has compassion on you."

Isaiah 54:10

Chapter 2
God is Our Strength

Day 8

"God is our refuge and strength, an ever-present help in trouble. Therefore, we will not fear, though the earth gives way and the mountains fall into the heart of the sea, though its waters roar and foam and the mountains quake with their surging."
Psalm 46:1-3

We must keep our minds at peace by reflecting on the promises of God. Nobody is more powerful than God and nothing can stop God's plans for our lives. Knowing these facts about God gives us peace. Having peace in God is our refuge.

Prayer:

Lord, thank You for giving us peace in You. Though at times we are uncertain, we can find refuge simply by thinking of Your Greatness. Thank you for casting out the fear in our hearts. In Jesus' name we pray, Amen.

Day 9

"My flesh and my heart may fail, but God is the strength of my heart and my portion forever."

Psalms 73:26

Most trials are spontaneous and will often catch us off guard. The truth of the matter is that most people appreciate and would much rather receive blessings over challenges and unfortunate situations. However, even when faced with unexpected tribulations, we must encourage ourselves through the promises of God. He is our strength whenever our flesh is weak.

Prayer:
Lord, thank You for Your promises. Although our flesh gets weak and we often fall short our strength is renewed whenever we reattach to You. Lord, give us a heart and mind to stay connected to You. In Jesus' name we pray, Amen.

Day 10

"I love you, LORD, my strength.

The Lord is my rock, my fortress and my deliverer; my God is my rock, in whom I take refuge, my shield and the horn of my salvation, my stronghold."

Psalms 18:1-2

Meditating on God's Word gives us strength. Keeping God on our mind keeps us from growing weary and it also helps us stay humble, understanding that we are nothing without Him. Knowing that our strength comes from God will cast out arrogance and fear. Our love for God will keep us reflecting on His greatness and not ourselves.

Prayer:

Lord, You are our rock and we love You. Father, help us to remember we can find refuge in You. In Jesus' name we pray, Amen.

Day 11

*"The LORD is good, a refuge in times of
trouble. He cares for those who trust in
him..."*

Nahum 1:7

As Believers, we must develop the ability to
get back into God's will whenever trials
come our way. God is our protector and He
will keep us from getting swallowed up in
our trials. Trusting God is vital for our
survival on Earth.

Prayer:

Lord, we desire to be Your representatives
on Earth. Father, thank You for calling us
out of darkness and teaching us how to take
refuge in Your Word. Lord, we trust You
and we'll continue to stand on Your Word in
our times of trouble. In Jesus' name we pray,
Amen.

Day 12

"Have I not commanded you? Be strong and courageous! Do not tremble or be dismayed, for the LORD your God is with you wherever you go."

Joshua 1:9

God left us commandments and instructions. It's important to read scriptures daily so that we develop a deeper understanding of who God is and bear witness to the fact that His Word still works. God's Word is alive and active in the life of every believer. The more we seek God; He reveals Himself to us and gives us boldness to stand on His Word.

Prayer:

Lord, thank You for revealing Yourself to us and giving us the courage needed for our journey. Lord, we love, trust and believe in You. Therefore, we will not tremble whenever we are faced with unforeseen obstacles. In Jesus' name we pray, Amen.

Day 13

*"Do not fear them, for the L*ORD *your God is the one fighting for you."*

Deuteronomy 3:22

Scriptures remind us of the fact that we are in a spiritual war. While it's true that God gave us dominion over everything on Earth, His Word also tells us that the battle is not ours. Our faith in God keeps us from fearing people. Knowledge in God increases our trust in God, which keeps us from fighting battles that are not ours.

Prayer:

Lord, thank You for increasing our faith and reminding us that the battle is not ours. Lord, we rest in you, trusting that you are protecting us from the attacks of the enemy. Lord, our faith in you keeps us from growing fearful of anything we witness going on around us. Father, thank You for fighting our battles. In Jesus' name we pray, Amen.

Day 14

"Be alert and of sober mind. Your enemy the devil prowls around like a roaring lion looking for someone to devour. Resist him, standing firm in the faith, because you know that the family of believers throughout the world is undergoing the same kind of sufferings. And the God of all grace, who called you to his eternal glory in Christ, after you have suffered a little while, will himself restore you and make you strong, firm and steadfast."

1 Peter 5:8-10

Sometimes we have difficulty analyzing whether or not God wants us to be still or flee from a particular trial that we are experiencing. This is why it is vital that we keep a sober mind so that we know how to respond whenever challenges are testing our faith.

The devil wants us dead so we cannot be caught off guard. We must understand that he will go to any length to destroy our lives. Reading scriptures; listening to inspirational music; watching motivational speakers;

singing praise and worship songs are some ways we can keep the devil from attacking us. Be encouraged to find ways to stay in God's presence.

Prayer:

Father, we know that the devil is under attack, but we also know that he cannot touch us whenever we are connected to You. Father help us to find ways to bask in Your presence. Father help us to create ways to enjoy You in our daily routines. In Jesus' name we pray, Amen.

"Sing to the LORD; praise his name. Each day proclaim the good news that he saves. Publish his glorious deeds among the nations. Tell everyone about the amazing things he does. Great is the LORD! He is most worthy of praise! He is to be feared above all gods."

Psalm 96:2-4

Chapter 3

What Are You Praying For?

Day 15

"If you abide in Me, and My words abide in you, ask whatever you wish, and it will be done for you."

John 15:7

God is constantly assisting us along our journey because He wants what's best for us. We lose track when we focus on things of this world rather than praying for things that God freely gives to us. His peace is far greater than any amount of money. Therefore, let's be encouraged to pray less for tangible things and more for things such as a clean spirit, gentleness, a loving and giving heart. These things will help us to develop the right spirit to serve God.

Prayer:

Lord, thank You for being so accessible to us. Father, keep our minds focused so that we don't lose hope when we're experiencing challenges. Lord, let Your Word abide in us so that we know how to stay in Your Will despite the challenges we experience from time to time. In Jesus' name we pray, Amen.

Day 16

*"God said to Solomon, 'Since this is your
heart's desire and you have not asked for
wealth, possessions or honor, nor for the
death of your enemies, and since you have
not asked for a long life but for wisdom and
knowledge to govern my people over whom I
have made you king, therefore wisdom and
knowledge will be given you. And I will also
give you wealth, possessions and honor,
such as no king who was before you ever
had and none after you will have.'"*

2 Chronicles 1:11-12

Whenever we walk in obedience to God's
Word, He blesses us, sometimes in ways we
never expect. In the scripture above, King
Solomon's prayer shows us the benefits of
remaining humble and seeking knowledge
and wisdom more over worldly things. Let
us take heed and adapt to the ways of
humble servants.

Prayer:
Father, thank You for Your willingness to
bless and honor our request. Lord, You are
awesome and we appreciate all the ways that

You bless our lives. Father, thank You. Lord, keep us humble so that we continue to seek Your face and do the things that are pleasing onto You. In Jesus' name we pray, Amen.

Day 17

"This is the confidence we have in approaching God: that if we ask anything according to his will, he hears us. And if we know that he hears us—whatever we ask— we know that we have what we asked of him."

1 John 5:14-15

Knowing God helps us to understand that His plan is what's best for us. God tells us to ask for what we want and He will give us the desires of our hearts. Therefore, we boldly go before God's throne making our request known. For God hears our prayers and He will bless our request according to His Will. When we live in obedience to God, we learn how to approach Him with confidence whenever we go to Him in prayer.

Prayer:

Lord, Thank You for building up our confidence in You. Father, help us to stay in Your will so that we request things that line up with Your plan for our lives. In Jesus' name we pray, Amen.

Day 18

"Do not be anxious about anything, but in every situation, by prayer and petition, with thanksgiving, present your requests to God. And the peace of God, which transcends all understanding, will guard your hearts and your minds in Christ Jesus."

Philippians 4:6-7

Stress and anxiety set in whenever our minds are consumed with worrisome thoughts. The peace of God can govern our lives and keep us from becoming stressed out or anxious if we allow Him. Let's be encouraged to pray to God to keep our minds undisturbed by the worries of the world.

Prayer:

Lord, thank You for giving us a chance to grow in grace. Father, we desire to represent You in all our ways. Lord, give us Your peace so that we don't become anxious during our journey. In Jesus' name we pray, Amen.

Day 19

"Therefore I tell you, whatever you ask for in prayer, believe that you have received it, and it will be yours."

Mark 11:24

The more we seek God, the more we will crave being in His presence. Being in God's presence will increase our faith as we develop in His Word. God's Word will help us to develop the right spirit for serving God. God's spirit will keep us humble and our prayers will not be in vain because God loves to bless His servants.

Prayer:

Lord, thank You for abiding in us and blessing us with Your spirit, which keeps our minds at peace in You. Lord, thank You for increasing our faith and for answering our prayers. In Jesus' name we pray, Amen.

Day 20

"Therefore confess your sins to each other and pray for each other so that you may be healed. The prayer of a righteous person is powerful and effective."
James 5:16

We all fall short. As new believers, we must help others on their journey by sharing our testimonies. Being honest about our shortcomings makes us relatable to others. This also can inspire them to start correcting their steps as well.

Sharing is important because more often than not people feel like outcasts. They simply don't realize how much they have in common with believers. While it's true that misery loves company, it's also true that people want to relate to and connect to God but some just don't know how. Sharing our journey with others creates a bridge that helps others relate to God as well.

Prayer:
Lord, thank You for blessing us with a mind to serve You. Father, as we witness so many lose their way, we desire to stand in the gap

for those lost souls. Lord, give us a sincere heart and compassion for others so that You can bless them through our prayers. In Jesus' name we pray, Amen.

Day 21

"Create in me a clean heart, O God, and renew a steadfast spirit within me."

Psalm 51:10

Before we can serve God wholeheartedly, we must be cleansed from sin. Our hearts and minds must be ready to serve God despite all or we will easily fall back into our old ways. Let us be encouraged to get serious about serving God so that we learn how to make our prayers intentional.

Prayer:

Father, as we witness Your Word coming to pass, we do not want to take Your grace and mercy for granted. Lord, forgive us for our sins and help us to develop Godly characteristics. Lord, we repent and turn from our wicked ways because we want to serve You wholeheartedly. Lord, clean us out and pour into us everything that will enable us to develop the right spirit so that we can represent You on Earth. In Jesus' name we pray, Amen.

*******REMINDER*******

"But seek first the kingdom of God and His righteousness, and all these things shall be added to you."

Matthew 6:33

Chapter 4
Letting Go of Sin

Day 22

"Whoever conceals their sins does not prosper, but the one who confesses and renounces them will find mercy."

Proverbs 28:13

There is no way we can correct our sins without first acknowledging that we are walking in error. Being healed and delivered can only take place after we admit our problems and surrender them to God. Our minds must be convinced that God's way is best. This will influence our decision to walk away from our old lifestyle.

Prayer:

Father, forgive us for our shortcomings and help us to abandon our old ways of thinking and living on Earth. Lord, we desire to get our lives in order. Thank You for giving us another opportunity to turn away from our crooked ways. In Jesus' name we pray, Amen.

Day 23

"In the past God overlooked such ignorance, but now he commands all people everywhere to repent."

Acts 17:30

Before we decided to repent and turn from our old ways, we were unaware of the ways of God. Now that we have renewed minds, we desire to please God with our lives. Therefore, we no longer walk in ignorance but in obedience. We've been influenced to turn away from our sins.

Prayer:

Lord, thank You for Your grace and mercy which has allowed us an opportunity to get our lives in order based on Your Word. Father, we realize that You expect more from us and command us to walk upright. Lord, forgive us for our sins and help us to walk in obedience to Your Word. In Jesus' name we pray, Amen.

Day 24

"Submit yourselves, then, to God. Resist the devil, and he will flee from you. Come near to God and he will come near to you. Wash your hands, you sinners, and purify your hearts, you double-minded."

James 4:7-8

Now that we've experienced God, it's not as easy for the devil to tempt us. However, as believers, we must stay out of environments where we will be influenced to sin. God tells us to resist the devil so we can no longer be around sinful people or go to the places where we will be influenced to sin. We must choose to be in environments that will allow us to draw closer to God.

Prayer:

Lord, we do not want to be double-minded hypocrites wandering in the wilderness being disobedient to Your Word. Father, forgive us for our stubborn ways which allowed us to walk comfortably in sin. Lord, cleanse us and purify our hearts so that we can draw closer to You. In Jesus' name we pray, Amen.

Day 25

"If we confess our sins, he is faithful and just and will forgive us our sins and purify us from all unrighteousness."

1 John 1:9

Confessing is admitting when we are wrong. Confession and repentance opens the door for God to bless us not rebuke us. Let's remember that God is faithful to those who are faithful to Him. Therefore, let's demonstrate a humble spirit that allows us to simply confess, repent and ask God for forgiveness daily.

Prayer:

Lord, forgive us for our sins and help us to become who You created us to be. Lord, cleanse us from all unrighteousness and strengthen us in the areas of our weaknesses so that we can represent You. In Jesus' name we pray, Amen.

Day 26

"Repent, then, and turn to God, so that your sins may be wiped out, that times of refreshing may come from the LORD"

Acts 3:19

Whenever we repent, we are refreshed. We can't function properly whenever we hold onto guilt over sins we've committed. The devil will try to remind us of our sins, but the Word of God tells us not to condemn ourselves. Therefore, now that we see the benefits of turning away from our wicked ways, we can't allow the devil to cause us to forget how refreshing it is to repent and turn to God.

Prayer:

Lord, forgive us for our sins. We want to be in Your will, but our flesh often causes us to fail. Lord, continue to bless us with a humble spirit so that we always have a mind to repent whenever we fall short. In Jesus' name we pray, Amen.

Day 27

*"Those whom I love I rebuke and discipline.
So be earnest and repent."*
Revelation 3:19

God loves us and wants the best for us.
Understanding God changes our perception
of life and sin. We belong to God, so our
lives are not our own. Our new mindset
helps us to accept and respect God's
discipline. God will continue to influence
and rebuke us whenever we are out of
order.

Prayer:

Lord, thank You for loving us and
constantly giving us opportunities to detach
from sin. Lord, we accept and respect Your
ways and desire to get it right. Father,
forgive us and continue to correct us. Reveal
to us our shortcomings whenever we are
walking in error. In Jesus's name we pray,
Amen.

Day 28

"For I take no pleasure in the death of anyone, declares the Sovereign LORD. Repent and live!"

Ezekiel 18:32

God does not want to release His wrath on us. He would much rather bless us, our lives with His loving kindness. This is why God is so patient with us. He continually gives us opportunities to repent and turn away from sin. God takes pleasure in pouring His blessings upon us.

Prayer:

Lord, thank You for being so patient with us. Father, we love You and we do not want to take Your grace and mercy for granted. Father forgive us for living carefree lives walking in disobedience. Lord, help us to earnestly seek You, so that we are never slow to repent and turn from our sins. In Jesus' name we pray, Amen.

43

Day 29

"...and call upon me in the day of trouble; I will deliver you, and you shall honor me."

Psalm 50:15

Throughout God's Word, He leaves us instructions on how to reconnect to Him. We must surrender our lives to Him so that letting go of sin becomes easier for us to do. Whenever we repent and call out to God, He will save us and deliver us from sin. Then, we will be strengthened and empowered to withstand the pressures of sin.

Prayer:

Lord, we need You. Father, thank you for teaching us how to call You in our hours of weakness. Lord, we need your guidance and protection, so we cry out to You. Thank you for being our present help in the times of troubles. Father, we desire to live glorifying You with our lives. Help us to become who You created us to be. In Jesus' name we pray, Amen.

Day 30

"I tell you, no! But unless you repent, you too will all perish."

Luke 13:3

When Jesus walked on Earth, He made it clear that He did not know when the end of the world as we know it would be. However, He did in fact give us all signs to look out for which indicated that the end was near. We can't take for granted God's warning signs. We must repent and turn to God or we will perish and spend eternity in Hell. Let's be clear, God does not require us to be perfect, but he commands us to repent and turn away from sin. Let's be encouraged to walk in obedience to God's Word.

Prayer:

Lord, although we don't have all the answers and have not fully adapted to your ways, we know that You are the answer and the only way. Lord, forgive us for our sins, cleanse us from all unrighteousness and fill us with Your Spirit so that we can walk in obedience to Your Word. In Jesus' name we pray, Amen.

*******REMINDER*******

"For sin shall not have any dominion over you, for you are not under law but under grace. What then? Shall we sin because we are not under law but under grace? Certainly not! Do you not know that to whom you present yourselves slaves to obey, you are that one's slaves whom you obey, whether of sin leading to death, or of obedience leading to righteousness? But God be thanked that though you were slaves of sin, yet you obeyed from the heart that form of doctrine to which you were delivered. And having been set free from sin, became slaves of righteousness."

Romans 6:14-18

Closing Remarks

I thank God for giving me a mind to share His Word with others. As a believer, I know it's vital to teach people how to seek God in these last and evil days.

While I can't relate to people who totally disregard God's Word, I can relate to not regarding God in all my ways, which is why it was easy for me to continue sinning early on in life. Thank God for deliverance.

Now that I have a mind to serve God, I desire to assist others in their quest to draw closer to God as well.

When I reflect on the days I was living in sin, I realize that I was comfortable because everybody around me was doing the same. I developed into a creature of my environment doing the things that made it evident that I was not living for God.

Following the ways of others kept me from trying to get to know God for myself. I spent the first half of my life listening to people's interpretation of who God was instead of trying to get to know Him for myself. This caused me to develop some form of an imaginary God in my head.

My prayer is that through reading, "Journey to Connecting with God", that others will be inspired to seek God for themselves as opposed to creating some form of an imaginary God in their mind.

God is real! When our perception about God is off, this keeps us from drawing closer to Him; which is why so many people are living comfortably in sin.

My prayer is that something in this book of devotionals inspires others to consider seeking God wholeheartedly for themselves. God is real and His Word is true and gives life to every believer.

May God continue to look after us, guide and protect us all from the wilds of this world. In Jesus' name I pray, Amen.

www.ingramcontent.com/pod-product-compliance
Lightning Source LLC
Chambersburg PA
CBHW061755040426
42447CB00011B/2315

9 7 8 0 9 9 8 1 1 0 3 5 6